Management Paper E2
Project and Relationship Management

Second edition 2015

ISBN 9781 4727 3431 0

e ISBN 9781 4727 3653 6

British Library Cataloguing-in-Publication Data

A catalogue record for this book is available from the British Library

Published by

BPP Learning Media Ltd,
BPP House, Aldine Place,
142-144 Uxbridge Road,
London W12 8AA

www.bpp.com/learningmedia

Printed in the United Kingdom
by Ashford

Unit 600
Fareham Reach
Gosport Hampsire
PO13 OFW

The contents of this book are intended as a guide and not
professional advice. Although every effort has been made to
ensure that the contents of this book are correct at the time of
going to press, BPP Learning Media makes no warranty that
the information in this book is accurate or complete and accept
no liability for any loss or damage suffered by any person
acting or refraining from acting as a result of the material in
this book.

Welcome to BPP Learning Media's CIMA **Passcards** for **Management Paper E2 Project and Relationship Management.**

- They **focus on your exam** and **save you time.**

- They incorporate **diagrams** to kickstart your memory.

- They follow the overall **structure** of the BPP Learning Media Study Texts, but BPP Learning Media's CIMA **Passcards** are not just a condensed book. Each card has been separately designed for clear presentation. Topics are self contained and can be grasped visually.

- CIMA **Passcards** are still **just the right size** for pockets, briefcases and bags.

Run through the **Passcards** as often as you can during your final revision period. The day before the exam, try to go through the **Passcards** again! You will then be well on your way to passing your exams.

Good luck!

Preface

Contents

1a: Introduction to strategy – Part A

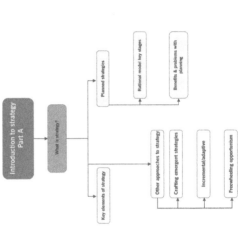

Strategy

A course of action, including the specification of resources required, to meet a specific objective.

Policy

Undated, long-lasting and often unquantified statement of guidance regarding the way organisations will seek to behave in relation to their stakeholders.

Tactics

The deployment of resources to execute an agreed strategy.

Strategic management

The development, implementation and control of agreed strategies.

Strategic plan

Statements of long-term goals along with the definition of the strategies and policies which will ensure achievements of these goals.

Levels of strategy

Corporate strategy 'is concerned with what **types of business** the company as a whole should be in and is therefore concerned with decisions of **scope**' *(Johnson and Scholes)*.

Business strategy defines how the organisation approaches a particular **market** or the activity of a particular **business unit**.

Operational and functional strategies are made at operational level in order to implement corporate and business strategies.

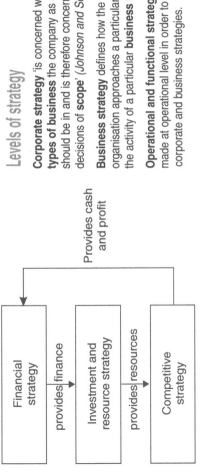

Financial strategy

provides finance

Investment and resource strategy

Provides cash and profit

provides resources

Competitive strategy

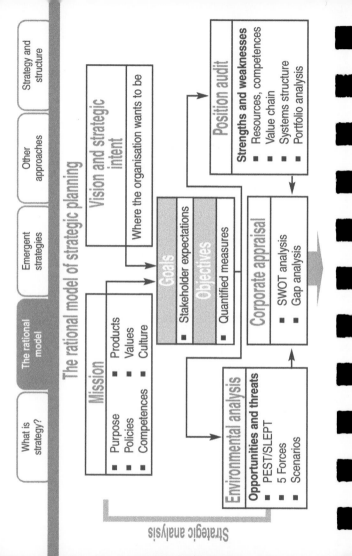

The rational model of strategic planning

| What is strategy? | The rational model | Emergent strategies | Other approaches | Strategy and structure |

Mission
- Purpose
- Policies
- Competences
- Products
- Values
- Culture

Vision and strategic intent

Where the organisation wants to be

Goals
- Stakeholder expectations

Objectives
- Quantified measures

Environmental analysis

Opportunities and threats
- PEST/SLEPT
- 5 Forces
- Scenarios

Position audit

Strengths and weaknesses
- Resources, competences
- Value chain
- Systems structure
- Portfolio analysis

Corporate appraisal
- SWOT analysis
- Gap analysis

Strategic analysis

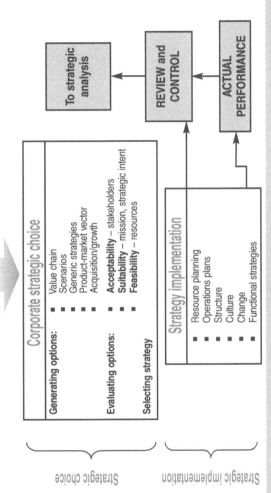

Corporate strategic choice

Generating options:
- Value chain
- Scenarios
- Generic strategies
- Product-market vector
- Acquisition/growth

Evaluating options:
- **Acceptability** – stakeholders
- **Suitability** – mission, strategic intent
- **Feasibility** – resources

Selecting strategy

Strategy implementation
- Resource planning
- Operations plans
- Structure
- Culture
- Change
- Functional strategies

To strategic analysis

REVIEW and CONTROL

ACTUAL PERFORMANCE

Strategic choice

Strategic implementation

For and against the rational model

For

- Identifies risks
- Forces managers to think
- Forces decision-making
- Formal targets enable control
- Enforces organisational coherence and co-ordination

Against

- Not proven to bring advantage
- May become over formal and reduce initiative
- Assumes internal politics do not exist
- Assumes managers know everything
- Divorces planning from doing
- Cannot cope with shocks and discontinuities

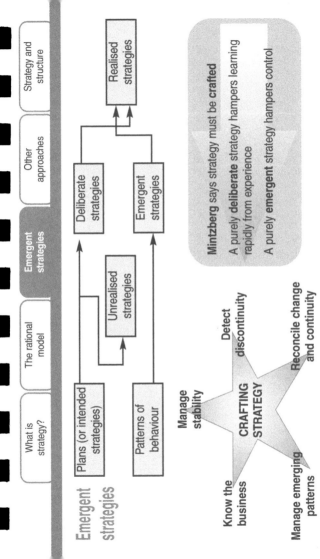

Emergent strategies

Plans (or intended strategies) → Deliberate strategies

Plans (or intended strategies) → Unrealised strategies

Unrealised strategies

Patterns of behaviour → Emergent strategies

Deliberate strategies → Realised strategies

Emergent strategies → Realised strategies

Mintzberg says strategy must be **crafted**

A purely **deliberate** strategy hampers learning rapidly from experience

A purely **emergent** strategy hampers control

CRAFTING STRATEGY

Detect discontinuity

Manage stability

Reconcile change and continuity

Know the business

Manage emerging patterns

1a: Introduction to strategy – Part A

Bounded rationality

Strategic managers' decision making is constrained by the time and amount of information available to them and by their own skills, habits and awareness.

They:

- Do **not** consider all options, but choose from a restricted range
- Make political compromises by **partisan mutual adjustment**
- **Satisfice** rather than optimise

Freewheeling opportunism

Suggests firms should not bother with strategic plans and should exploit opportunities as they arise.

Incrementalism

Development by small scale extensions of past practices.

This approach avoids major errors by the exercise of caution and produces acceptable solutions because it uses consultation, compromise and accommodation.

Logical incrementalism combines this approach with an in-depth review to establish the broad outlines of strategy.

Renewal	
☑ Creativity	☑ Trust
☑ Learning	☑ Support
☑ Initiative	

Strategy Safari

In the book 'Strategy Safari: The Complete Guide through the Wilds of Strategic Management', Mintzberg, Ahlstrand and Lampel outline ten different schools of thought to the process of strategic development.

10 schools

- The design school
- The planning school
- The positioning school
- The entrepreneurial school
- The cognitive school

- The learning school
- The power school
- The cultural school
- The environmental school
- The configuration school

Mintzberg, Ahlstrand and Lampel do not claim that one particular approach to strategy development is best. Their work simply offers a range of different ways in which organisations may approach the process of strategic development.

Structure is an important aspect of the implementation of strategy and should be optimised to support the overall strategic approach.

Significant strategic considerations

- Large size plus diversified products
- Project based production
- Stable environment and activity, need for expertise and precision
- Innovation, unstable environment

Possible structural response

- Divisionalised form
- Matrix; adhocracy
- Bureaucracy, machine or professional
- Simple form

1b: Introduction to strategy – Part B

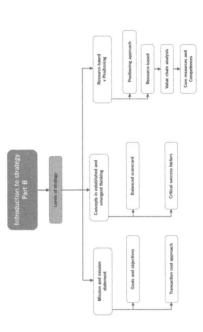

Positioning approach and resource-based approach

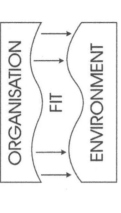

Rational model
Emergent model
Incrementalism
Ecology model

ALL about **positioning** to create competitive advantage:

In contrast, the **resource-based approach** suggests that the environment is too uncertain for this to work and that competitive advantage comes from the possession of **unique resources.**

- **Scarce resources** (eg intellectual property, raw materials, brand)
- **Core competences** are those that both out perform competitors and are difficult to imitate. They can be very specialised.

Four point criteria

Barney (1991) proposed the following four point criteria when evaluating the value of an organisation's **unique resources**.

Four point criteria

- Valuable
- Rare
- Imperfectly imitable
- Substitutability

Distinctive capabilities

Resource-based theorists have attempted to identify where internal competitive advantage comes from. **Kay (1997)** suggests that competitive advantage comes from a combination of:

- **Competitive architecture.** This refers to the relationships that make up the organisation.

- **Reputation.** This refers to the standing that the organisation has created among key stakeholders including customers, suppliers and investors.

- **Innovative ability.** This is concerned with developing new products and services.

- **Possession of strategic assets.** This refers to those unique resources and competences that the organisation may have.

How to organise production?

Market basis ← → Hierarchy basis

Transaction costs

Costs associated with **contracts**

Costs associated with premises, services, employment, administration

Problems

Uncertainty due to change makes long-term contracts unsatisfactory. Short-term contracts increase costs. **Bounded Rationality** means that there is no perfect knowledge of these changes. **Asset specificity** (see next page).

Managers subvert mission and pursue personal or system goals. Monopolistic inefficiency, stagnation and inefficiency of overlarge and complex bureaucracy are other problems.

Asset specificity

Relationship-specific assets are assets which have little or no application outside of a specific commercial relationship.

Insights of the transaction cost approach

- Asset specificity drives **vertical integration** and thus the growth of organisations.
- Possession of vital **resources** and **core capabilities** can reduce cost and increase control.
- Likewise, **contracting for non-core services and supplies** can reduce cost and complexity.
- **Divisional form** of organisation can reduce extent of bureaucracy and subversion of mission.

Outsourcing or contracting for non-core services, is beneficial if it will save the company money.
A company should not, however, outsource the resources and competences which give it its competitive advantage.

Porter grouped the various activities of an organisation into a **value chain**.

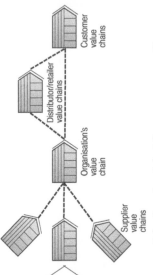

SUPPORT ACTIVITIES

FIRM INFRASTRUCTURE

HUMAN RESOURCE MANAGEMENT

TECHNOLOGY DEVELOPMENT

PROCUREMENT

| INBOUND LOGISTICS | OPERATIONS | OUTBOUND LOGISTICS | MARKETING & SALES | SERVICE |

MARGIN

MARGIN

PRIMARY ACTIVITIES

The **margin** is the excess the customer is prepared to **pay** over the **cost** to the firm of obtaining resource inputs and providing value activities. It represents the **value created** by the value **activities** themselves and by the **management of the linkages** between them. **Linkages** connect the activities in the value chain. The activities affect one another and therefore must be co-ordinated.

A firm's value chain is connected to what *Porter* calls a **value system**.

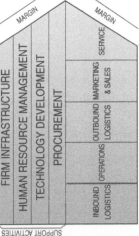

Supplier value chains

Organisation's value chain

Distributor/retailer value chains

Customer value chains

Using the value chain. A firm can secure competitive advantage in several ways.

- Invent new or better ways to do activities
- Combine activities in new or better ways
- Manage the linkages in its own value chain
- Manage the linkages in the value system

All organisations have a reason for existence. A clear statement of purpose is an important input into management at all levels.

Vision

The strategic thinker's idea of what the organisation could be in the future.

It must not ignore practical problems or degenerate into wishful thinking.

Strategic intent

A dream, to stretch and energise the organisation, to give a sense of direction and coherence to plans.

(Hamel and Prahalad)

Used to

Plan, evaluate and implement.

Mission

'The organisation's basic function in society'

(Mintzberg)

Includes, typically:

- **Purpose**
- Basic **strategy** eg products
- **Policies** and **standards of behaviour**
- **Values** and **culture**
  - Business principles
  - Internal relationships
  - Behaviour

Goals and Objectives

Goals and objectives flow from mission. The terminology is not standardised.

They should balance:
- Long term considerations
- Short term imperatives

They should be **consistent** across the organisation so that all pull together

They should be:
- Specific
- Measurable
- Attainable
- Results oriented
- Time bounded

MBO Where goals are broken down into targets for departments and individuals.

CSF Those factors which are essential and effective in delivering competitive advantage.

Hierarchy of objectives

For a commercial organisation, the highest level of objective will always be based on **profitability** over the long term, though **growth** may be regarded as of equal importance.

Secondary objectives include functional and departmental objectives as well as corporate objectives that support the main objective.

How to deal with conflict between the demands of secondary objectives

- **Bargaining** between managers
- **Satisficing** ie satisfactory rather than ideal performance
- **Sequential attention** to goals in turn
- **Priority setting** by senior managers

Kaplan and Norton suggest a **balanced scorecard** for measuring performance. This is also a valid approach to setting objectives: business must work towards achievement in four **perspectives.**

- Financial performance
- Internal systems and methods
- Customer satisfaction
- Innovation and learning

Implementation requires detailed planning and management of resources and operations.

Resource planning

1. **Resource audit** establishes currently available or obtainable resources.

2. **Estimate resources** required for strategy and whether those available are adequate.

3. **Assign responsibility** to managers for acquisition, use and control of resources.

4. **Identify constraints** and influences on availability and use of resources.

Detailed plans are made in light of:

- **Critical success factors**
- **Key tasks**
- **Priorities**

Operations planning

1. **Decide** what is to be done, by whom, when and at what cost.

2. Set up **control points** and methods of monitoring performance.

Review and control

- **Implementation** remains the responsibility of senior managers.

- **Control** should deal with deadlines, targets, resources, products and markets.

- **Control systems** must be designed in detail.

2: General environment

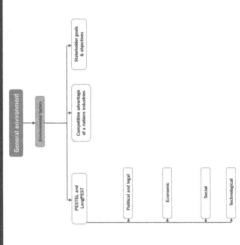

General environment

Environmental factors

PESTEL and LongPEST | Competitive advantage of a nations industries | Stakeholder goals & objectives

Political and legal

Economic

Social

Technological

One important approach to making strategy is seeking a good fit with the environment.

The impact of uncertainty

Complexity + dynamism = uncertainty:

Complexity

- Variety of influences
- Interconnectedness

Dynamism

- Pace of change

High uncertainty leads to:

- Desire for more **information**
- **Conservative** strategy with some **emergent** strategy
- Close planning time horizon

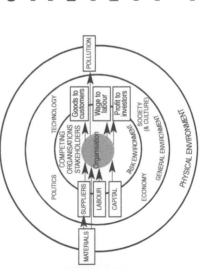

A framework for analysing the environment is PEST.

Political/legal factors

Many aspects of business activity are subject to legal regulation:

- Contract
- Health and safety
- Data protection
- Employment
- Tax
- Consumer protection

Other aspects are regulated by supervisory bodies. The EU is a significant influence.

Economic factors

These operate in both a national and international context. Relevant factors include:

- Inflation rates
- Employment rates
- Interest rates
- Capital markets
- Savings levels
- Exchange rates
- The business cycle
- International trade

Government policy

- Fiscal policy (taxes, borrowing, spending)
- Monetary policy (interest rates, exchange rates)
- Size and scope of the public sector

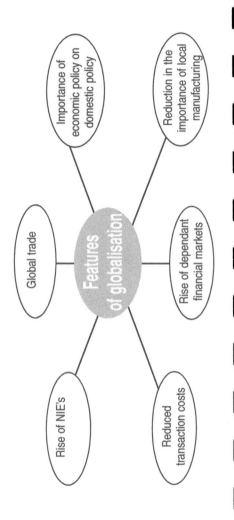

Globalisation refers to the growing interdependence of countries worldwide through increased trade, increased capital flows and the rapid diffusion of technology.

Features of globalisation

- Importance of economic policy on domestic policy
- Reduction in the importance of local manufacturing
- Rise of dependant financial markets
- Reduced transaction costs
- Rise of NIE's
- Global trade

Technological factors

Many strategies are based on exploiting technological change (eg Internet trading). Others are defences against such change (eg emphasising service or quality when a competitor introduces a major technical development).

Technological developments affect all aspects of business (especially IT developments)

- New products and services become available
- New methods of production and service provision
- Improved handling of information in sales and finance
- New organisation structures to exploit technology
- New media for communication with customers and within the business (eg Internet)

Social factors

Demography is the study of human population and population trends.

Demographic factors such as birth rate, average age, ethnicity, death rate, family structure have clear implications for patterns of demand and availability of labour.

Culture in society is as important as organisational culture in a business.

Cultural factors include language, religion, custom, music and literature. TV is a vital aspect in culture. Business must be particularly aware of **cultural change.**

LoNG PEST analysis

- The PESTEL Framework can be extended to create a LoNGPEST analysis.

- A LoNGPEST analysis views PESTEL factors at three different levels:

    – Local
    – National
    – Global

- LoNGPEST analysis helps management to better understand key external influences.

| Competitive advantage of nations |
| Stakeholders |
| PESTEL factors/LoNGPEST |
| The organisation and its environment |

Stakeholders' interests are likely to conflict. *Mendelow's* **stakeholder mapping** helps the organisation to establish its priorities and manage stakeholder expectations.

- **A:** Minimal effort
- **B: Keep informed**; little direct influence but may influence more powerful stakeholders
- **C:** Treat with care; often passive but capable of moving to segment D; **keep satisfied**
- **D:** Key players – strategy must be **acceptable** to them, at least

Level of interest

	Low	High
Power Low	A	B
High	C	D

Stakeholders

Groups or individuals who have an interest in an organisation's strategy.

Internal Employees, management

Connected Owners, suppliers, customers, lenders

OR

External Government, local communities

Primary Have contractual relationship

Secondary Do not

(Primary = Internal + Connected)

Porter identifies four determinants of national competitive advantage on an industry basis. He refers to it as the 'diamond'.

Firm strategy, structure and rivalry

Cultural factors, time horizons, capital markets and response to recession all help determine orientation and capability. Rivalry leads to competitive strength.

Demand conditions

Home market buyers set fundamental parameters such as market segments, degree of sophistication, rate of growth and rate of innovation. Early saturation of the home market will encourage a firm to export.

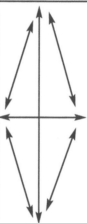

Factor conditions

Endowments of inputs to production
Basic: natural resources, climate, labour – unsustainable for competitive advantage
Advanced: infrastructure, technical education, high tech industries – promote competitive advantage

Related and supporting industries

Success in related industries gives mutual support. Strong home suppliers make the industry more robust. Rivalry creates supplier specialisations. **Clusters** of related industries derive strength from their links.

The economies of **Newly Industrialising and Emerging nations** (NIEs) have grown significantly in recent years. These countries are becoming increasingly important in World Politics.

Four significant emerging economies are the BRIC nations, Brazil, Russia, India and China.

BRIC economies

- China is currently the second largest economy in the world.

- When combined, BRIC nations have a larger share of world trade than the U.S.

There are four main types of economic system in operation in the world.

Economic systems

- Planned economy
- Free Market economy
- Mixed economy
- Transition economy

Types of economic system

Emerging economies

Successful emerging nations follow three main strategies:

- Export of natural commodities – eg precious metals such as gold

- Import-substitution – eg invest in new industries which produce more advanced products

- Export – led industrialisation – eg increase exports

2: General environment

Notes

3: Competitive environment

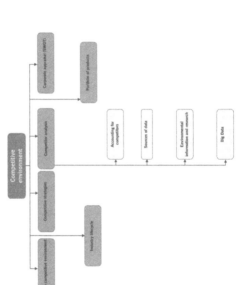

The purpose of analysing competitors is to try to predict what they might do, and what they cannot do.

Competitor intelligence systems

Situation, strategy and capability

Overall capability and cost competences

Assumptions

What it believes about the industry

Competitor response profile

This indicates the competitor's vulnerability and the most appropriate 'battleground'.

Competitor's goals

- Financial targets
- Risk assessments
- Organisational structure

Barriers to entry

Low barriers permit competitors to enter market – potential losses from competition may make cost of raising barriers worthwhile – eg by brand-building advertising campaign.

Sources of information

- Financial statements
- Customers and suppliers
- Products
- Former employees
- Job advertisements

The management accountant's role

- Analyse relative costs
- Analyse market share
- Cost structure
- Competitor behaviour

1 Strategic planning

- Information about the environment (PEST)
- Internal data (eg profitability, cost of funds, investment requirements)

Information

The information required embraces the entire organisation and provides a comparison between actual results and the plan.

2 Management control

All the processes used by managers to ensure that organisational goals are achieved and procedures adhered to, and that the organisation responds appropriately to changes in the environment.

3 Operational control

Information needed to conduct day-to-day implementation of plans – largely details of individual transactions.

Risk

Involves situation or events which may or may not occur, but whose probability of occurrence can be calculated statistically and the frequency of their occurrence predicted from past records.

Uncertainty

Involves events whose outcome *cannot* be predicted with statistical confidence.

An event will be risky or uncertain depending on whether or not sufficient information is available to allow the lack of certainty to be quantified. As a rule, however, the terms are used interchangeably.

Decision making

Problem recognition

Problem definition

Identify alternative courses of action

Make the decision

Implement the decision

Monitor the outcome

Amend decision

More information

Strategic intelligence

is what a firm needs to know about its environment to enable it to anticipate change and design appropriate strategies.

Creating strategic intelligence

External sources

- The press
- Trade associations
- Trade publications
- Government departments
- Internet
- Public databases

Collected from relevant and meaningful sources

Internal sources

- Sales force
- Market research
- Management information system
- Databases

After the information has been collected, it needs to be organised, analysed, communicated and finally used as strategic intelligence.

Database information

A database

is a collection of data organised to service many applications and provides data for a wide range of uses and needs.

Big data

is a popular term used to describe the exponential growth and availability of data, both structured and unstructured. Big data may be as important to business and society as the internet has become (www.sas.com).

Laney's 3V's of big data

- Volume
- Velocity
- Variety

Competitive strategies

Competitive strategy means taking offensive or defensive actions to create a dependable position in an industry, to cope successfully with competitive forces and thereby yield a superior return on investment for the firm. (*Porter*)

Porter believes there are three **generic strategies** for competitive advantage:

- **Cost leadership** means being the lowest cost producer in the industry as a whole.
- **Differentiation** is the exploitation of a product or service that the **industry as a whole** believes to be unique.
- **Focus** involves a restriction of activities to only part of the market (a segment) through:

  – Providing goods and/or services at lower cost to that segment (**cost-focus**)

  – Providing a differentiated product or service to that segment (**differentiation-focus**)

The strategy clock

The strategy clock develops Porter's theory, analysing strategies in terms of **price and perceived value added**.

The eight strategies shown on the clock represent different approaches to creating value for the customer. Each customer will buy from the provider whose offering most closely matches their own view of the proper relationship between price and perceived benefits.

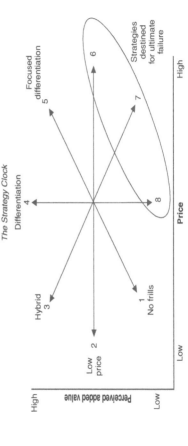

The Strategy Clock

Product-market strategy: direction of growth

Product-market strategies involve determining which products should be sold in which markets.

Product-market mix

Ansoff drew up a **growth vector matrix**, describing how a combination of a firm's activities in current and new markets, with existing and new products can lead to growth.

- Existing products and existing markets: **market penetration**
- Existing products and new markets: **market development**
- New products and existing markets: **product development**
- New products: new markets **(diversification)**

Ansoff's competitive strategies (Ansoff matrix)

	Products	
	Existing	New
Existing	Market Penetration	Product Development
New	Market Development	Diversification

Markets

Method of growth

Once an organisation has selected an appropriate competitive strategy, consideration needs to be given to the method it will use to deliver it.

Different methods of growth

- **Organic growth** (sometimes referred to as internal development) is achieved through the development of internal resources.

- **Acquisition** involves growing through buying another organisation.

- **Joint ventures** involve two firms (or more) joining forces and establishing a separate new entity with each partner holding a share in both the equity and the management of the business.

- **Alliances** involve firms entering into long-term strategic alliances with other organisations. This can be for a variety of reasons including sharing development costs, to learn from each other or to complement each others product offering.

Porter says that **five forces** together determine the long term profit potential of an industry

3 Bargaining power of customers

Depends on:

- Volume bought
- Scope for substitution
- Switching costs
- Purchasing skills
- Importance of quality

2 Threat of new entrants

This is limited by **barriers to entry**

- Scale economies
- Switching costs
- Patent rights
- Product differentiation
- Access to distribution
- Access to resources

4 Rivalry among current competitors

Depends on:

- Market growth
- Spare capacity
- Uncertainty about competitor's strategy
- Buyers ease of switching
- Exit barriers

5 Threat from substitute products

A substitute is produced by a different industry but satisfies the same needs.

1 Bargaining power of suppliers

Depends on:

- Number of suppliers
- Threats to suppliers industry
- Number of customers in the industry
- Scope for substitution
- Switching costs
- Selling skills

Customers seek lower prices

Suppliers seek higher prices

4: Key concepts in management

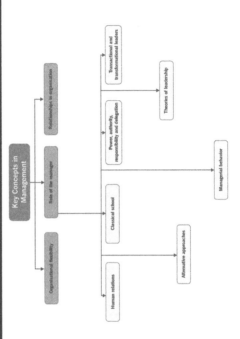

Key Concepts in Management

- Organisational flexibility
- Role of the manager
- Relationships in organisation

Role of the manager:
- Human relations
- Classical school
- Power, authority, responsibility and delegation
- Transactional and transformational leaders

- Alternative approaches
- Managerial behavior
- Theories of leadership

Why are managers needed?

- **Objectives** must be set and then achieved
- **Corporate values** must be sustained
- **Key stakeholders** must be satisfied

What do managers do?

Fayol: the classical school

- **Planning:** objectives and methods
- **Organising:** task structure, organisation structure, feed back
- **Commanding:** giving instructions
- **Co-ordinating:** individual and group activities
- **Controlling:** checking performance and taking corrective action

Taylor: scientific management

The essence of Taylor's approach was **efficiency** in an engineering sense. He treated work people as tools to be used efficiently. (Note that this includes caring for them properly.)

Practical implications

- **Work study** establishes the 'one best way' – no discretion is allowed to the worker.
- **Work planning** is done by a separate team of experts.
- **Pay incentives** are used to motivate on the basis of increased output.
- The **work environment** is set up so as to enable the greatest efficiency.

Drucker: management process and MBO

- Setting objectives
- Organising the work
- Motivating
- Measuring results
- Developing people

Management of *commercial* enterprises has an extra fundamental responsibility: **economic performance.**

- **Managing a business:** marketing and innovation
- **Managing managers:** management by objectives (MBO)
- **Managing workers and work**

Management and subordinate agree **measurable objectives** for performance that supports the organisation's mission. Regular **feedback** on attainment supports **improved performance.**

Elton Mayo: human relations

- **Western Electric – Hawthorne studies: worker attitudes** and **group relations** affected production more than conditions.

  People are motivated by a variety of **psychological needs** including **social** needs.

- **Maslow and Herzberg: Neo-human relations:** workers have 'higher-order' needs including personal development.

  This approach stresses the impact of human behaviour in the group and on organisational performance.

Mintzberg: what managers actually do:

- **Interpersonal roles:** hiring, firing, training, motivating, liaising

- **Informational roles:** the manager has many contacts inside and outside the department and organisation; he **monitors** the environment, disseminates information, acts as a spokesman

- **Decisional roles:**
  - **Entrepreneur,** initiating action
  - **Disturbance handler,** resolving the unpredictable
  - **Allocator of source resources**
  - **Negotiator**

Authority is the right to act in a given context: *power* confers the ability to act.

Sources of power (French and Raven)

- **Coercive power** is power based on the ability to impose sanctions.

- **Resource power** depends on the control of resources; managers may utilise this by controlling **rewards** and access to information.

- **Position** or **legitimate power** stems from status or appointment within an organisation and is thus equivalent to **authority**.

- **Expert power** flows from acknowledged expertise.

- **Referent power** lies in the personal qualities of the individual. It can be important in the workings of the informal organisation.

- **Negative power** lies in the ability to prevent or disrupt proposed action.

Authority

is the **right** to do something, or to ask someone else to do it and expect it to be done.

- **Line authority**: a manager has line authority over a direct subordinate.
- **Functional authority**: specialist managers have authority to issue instructions concerning their own areas of responsibility to managers and members of other departments.
- **Staff or advisory authority** is the authority a specialist manager has to give **advice** to other departments.

Responsibility

is the **obligation** a person has to fulfil a task he has been given.

Delegation

Senior managers **delegate** authority to subordinate managers so that they can be **responsible** for specific aspects of the senior managers' spheres of activity. The juniors are **accountable** to the seniors for their responsibility but the seniors **remain fully accountable** to their own superiors. Authority can be delegated, but **not** accountability.

Accountability

is a person's **liability** to be called to account for the fulfilment of tasks he has been given.

Empowerment

is where workers are responsible for achieving and even setting work targets, with the freedom to decide how they are achieved.

Management

- Copes with complexity
- Prescribed role and status
- Maintaining status quo
- Secure compliance with organisational objectives
- Over resources

Leadership

- Copes with change
- Through perception of others as followers
- New approaches and ideas
- **Influences** others to fulfil organisational objectives
- Over people

Transactional leaders

Exchange rewards in return for service, loyalty and compliance

Transformational leaders

Impact and motivate others

4: Key concepts in management

| Role of the manager | Authority relationships | Leadership | Discipline, grievance and termination | Equal opportunities and diversity |

1. Style approaches to leadership

THE SPECTRUM OF MANAGEMENT STYLES

Authoritarian Task ←→ **Democratic Relationship**

| Manager makes decisions and enforces them | Manager 'sells' his decisions to subordinates | Manager suggests own ideas and asks for comments | Manager sketches ideas, asks for comments and amends his ideas | Manager presents a problem, asks for ideas, makes a decision from the ideas | Manager presents a problem to subordinates and asks them to solve it | Manager allows his subordinates to act as they wish within specified limits |

(Tannenbaum and Schmidt)

Theory X

People dislike work and must be coerced into doing it.

Theory Y

Work is as natural as play or rest and can be satisfying.

(McGregor)

Likert's four management 'systems'

Exploitative authoritative	Benevolent authoritative	Consultative	Participative
- No confidence or trust in subordinates - Decisions imposed - No delegation of decision-making - Threats used to motivate - Little communication or teamwork with subordinates	- Superficial, condescending confidence and trust - Decisions imposed - Rewards used to motivate - Paternalistic involvement of subordinates	- Substantial confidence and trust in subordinates - Consults but controls decision-making - Some motivation by involvement - Uses subordinates' ideas	- Great trust in subordinates - Delegation of decision-making - Goals set participatively, achievement rewarded - Ideas and opinions shared

(Likert)

Likert suggested that effective managers naturally use **participative** or **consultative** styles.

Ashridge Management College studies found a similar spread. Their model is tabulated on the next two pages. Note particularly that this model summarises the strengths and weaknesses of the various styles: these may be applied to the models above.

4: Key concepts in management

Ashridge Management College model

Style	Characteristics	Strengths	Weaknesses
Tells (autocratic)	The manager makes all the decisions, and issues instructions which must be obeyed without question.	(1) Quick decisions can be made when speed is required. (2) It is the most efficient type of leadership for highly-programmed routine work.	(1) Quick decisions can be made when speed is required. (2) It does not encourage initiative and commitment from subordinates.
Sells (persuasive)	The manager still makes all the decisions, but believes that subordinates have to be motivated to accept them in order to carry them out properly.	(1) Employees are made aware of the reasons for decisions. (2) Selling decisions to staff might make them more committed. (3) Staff will have a better ideas of what to do when unforeseen events arise in their work because the manager will have explained his intentions.	(1) Communications are still largely one-way. Sub-ordinates might not accept the decisions. (2) It does not encourage initiative and commitment from subordinates.

Ashridge Management College model cont.

Consults	The manager confers with subordinates and takes their views into account, but has the final say.	(1) Employees are involved in decisions before they are made. This encourages motivation through greater interest and involvement. (2) An agreed consensus of opinion can be reached and for some decisions consensus can be an advantage rather than a weak compromise. (3) Employees can contribute their knowledge and experience to help in solving more complex problems.	(1) It might take much longer to reach the decisions. (2) Subordinates might be too inexperienced to formulate mature opinions and give practical advice. (3) Consultation can too easily turn into a facade concealing, basically, a sells style.
Joins (democratic)	Leader and followers make the decision on the basis of consensus.	(1) It can provide high motivation and commitment from employees. (2) It shares the other advantages of the consultative style (especially where subordinates have expert power).	(1) The authority of the manager might be undermined. (2) Decision-making might become a very long process, and clear decisions might be difficult to reach. (3) Subordinates might lack enough experience.

The Managerial Grid (Blake and Mouton)

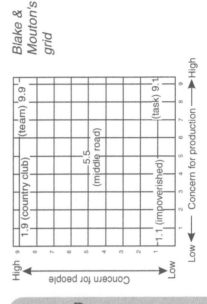

Blake & Mouton's grid

Extreme cases

1.1 impoverished: manager is lazy: little interest in either staff or work

1.9 country club: manager attentive to staff needs, has developed satisfying relationships: little attention to achieving results

9.1 task management: almost total concentration on achieving results. People's needs are virtually ignored

5.5 middle of the road: adequate performance balancing work results with maintaining satisfactory morale

9.9 team: high work accomplishment through leading committed people

2. Contingency approaches to leadership

Appropriateness of action depends on the circumstances.

Action-centred leadership (Adair)

Leadership activities must satisfy 3 sets of varying needs in accordance with the priorities inherent in the prevailing situation. Leadership lies in performing leadership functions or roles related to the 3 sets of needs. Adair rejects the notion that leadership depends on inherent personal qualities.

Group maintenance roles	Task roles	Individual maintenance roles
■ Encouraging peace-keeping, Clarifying, Standard-setting	■ Initiating, Information-seeking, Diagnosing, Opinion-seeking, Evaluating, Decision-making	■ Goal-setting, Feedback Recognition, Counselling, Training

4: Key concepts in management

Situational leadership (*Hershey and Blanchard*)

Team members are ranked on **ability** and **willingness** to complete a task successfully. Based on this, managers need to **adapt their leadership style**. There are **four** types of team:

1. **High – readiness.** Able and willing. The most appropriate leadership style here is **delegation**.

2. **High – moderate readiness.** Able but unwilling or insecure. A manager needs to be supportive and the most appropriate style is **participating.**

3. **Low – moderate readiness.** Lack ability but are willing and confident. A manager needs to be directive and supportive. The most appropriate style is **selling.**

4. **Low-readiness.** Lack ability and confidence. A manager needs to be directive and so the most appropriate management style is **telling.**

Fiedler's contingency model

Fiedler investigated the link between leadership and organisational performance. He found that style of leadership could be linked to the extent to which the situation was favourable or unfavourable, as determined by 3 main factors:

- **Position power** is the degree of formal authority possessed by the manager.

- **Task structure**: clear, unambiguous tasks are easier to control than vague unstructured ones.

- **Leader – subordinate relations**: trust and confidence in the manager ease his task.

The 3 variables determine the ease with which the manager can influence subordinates' behaviour. The implications for management style are shown below.

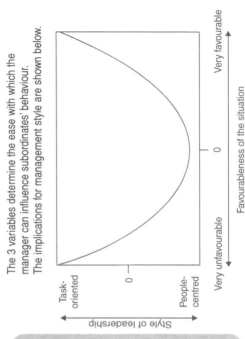

Discipline

Positive: aid safety and successful completion of tasks.

Negative: sanctions designed to make people choose to behave in a desirable way.

ACAS Code of Practice

In the UK, discipline in most organisations is governed by the ACAS Code of Practice. This specifies the requirements of good disciplinary procedures (eg they should be in writing; they should be non-discriminatory) and lays down how disciplinary incidents should be dealt with.

- Any incident must be **thoroughly investigated** and a written record made. Minor cases are disposed of informally.

- **First warning**: oral or written depending on the gravity of the case. A first written warning is also appropriate when a first oral warning has been disregarded.

- **Final written warning**: warns of punitive action and explains appeal procedure.

Formal warnings have a limited period of validity, eg 12 months.

Employment Act 2002

A **statutory disciplinary procedure** was introduced in the UK on 1 October 2004.

1. Manager writes to employee inviting attendance at meeting to discuss matter. Employee has right to be accompanied.

2. At meeting manager explains problem and invites response. After meeting manager explains decision and right of appeal.

3. Employee may appeal to more senior, or, at least, different, manager and has right to be accompanied at appeal.

Disciplinary sanctions

Sanctions should be:

- **Immediate:** very difficult if the ACAS procedure is followed.
- **Consistent:** subject to mitigating circumstances, an offence should always be treated the same way.
- **Impersonal:** no element of personal malice or favour should appear.

There should also be **advance warning** (eg in induction training) so that everyone knows what to expect.

UK statutory grievance procedure

From 1 **October 2004**.

1 Employee sets out grievance in writing.

2 Meeting: employee has right to be accompanied. Manager announces decision and informs employee of right of appeal.

3 Employee may appeal to more senior, or, at least, different, manager and has right to be accompanied.

Potentially fair grounds for dismissal

- **Redundancy**: selection must be fair
- **Legal impediment**: retention would break the law (eg a struck-off doctor)
- Inadequate **capability**, provided training and warnings have been given
- **Misconduct** after adequate warning
- **Other substantial reason**

Automatically unfair grounds for dismissal

- Unfair selection for redundancy
- Trade union activity or membership
- Pregnancy
- Certain health and safety related activities
- Insisting on documented employment particulars or payslips

Termination of employment

Dismissal includes:

1. **Termination** of an employee's contract by the employer

2. The ending of a **fixed term contract** without renewal of the same terms

3. Resignation when the employer's conduct breaches the contract of employment: this is **constructive dismissal.**

Redundancy

Is defined as **dismissal** when:

The employer has **ceased business** or part of business where the employee worked.

The **requirements** for particular work have **ceased or diminished** or are expected to.

Wrongful dismissal

Wrongful dismissal is dismissal that breaches the terms of the contract of employment (eg if inadequate notice is given).

Unfair dismissal

Unfair dismissal is any dismissal that does not fall into the statutorily defined categories of fair dismissal. Some dismissals are automatically unfair.

Discrimination

Direct discrimination: one group is treated less favourably than another.

Indirect discrimination: a substantial proportion of a group cannot comply with requirements or conditions, to their detriment.

Positive discrimination gives preference to a protected group.

Sexual harassment

Sexual harassment is any unwanted conduct with sexual connotations. In the UK, most sexual harassment is likely to constitute unlawful sex discrimination.

Diversity

Equal opportunities is about removing unfair discrimination. **Diversity** as a concept is about taking advantage of heterogeneity in order to thrive in a diverse global business environment.

The Equality Act (2010)

The **Equality Act (2010)** is a piece of legislation governing equal treatment in the workplace. It has reduced the need for a vast array of complicated laws and regulations. The Equality Act (2010) has extended the range of protected characteristics which employers must abide by:

- Sex
- Sexual orientation
- Religion or belief
- Race
- Pregnancy and maternity
- Marriage and civil partnership
- Gender reassignment
- Disability
- Age

Equal opportunity in recruitment

- **Advertising material** must not indicate any discriminatory preference nor may its distribution restrict its availability to preferred groups.

- **Application forms** and **interviews** must not ask non-work related questions.

- **Selection tests** should be culturally non-specific.

- **Rejection**: reasons should be recorded.

Management of equal opportunities

- **Support from the top** is needed.

- A **policy on equal opportunities** is helpful, perhaps prepared by a **working party** with wide representation.

- **Monitoring**: applications, starters, leavers, transfers, promotions and training should be monitored for their impact on disadvantaged groups.

- **Resources** will be needed for practical action, which might include:
  - Flexible work patterns for women
  - Equal opportunities managers
  - Awareness training for managers
  - Childcare arrangements
  - Encouragement of job applications from members of disadvantaged groups

5: Culture

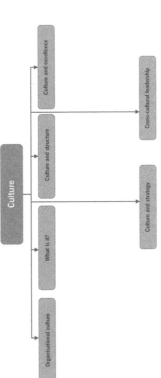

Culture
- Organisational culture
- What is it?
- Culture and structure
- Culture and excellence
- Cross-cultural leadership
- Culture and strategy

Culture

> Culture in an organisation is the sum of the beliefs, assumptions, attitudes, customs and practices to which people are exposed during their interaction with the organisation. *Schein* referred to it as 'The way we do things round here.'

The organisational structure exists within the wider cultural setting of the society it is part of, since the people involved are members of both.

Different aspects of an organisation's culture are manifested in different parts of the organisation. **Position in the hierarchy** is a particularly important determinant of sub-cultural values.

The 'organisational iceberg'

Overt aspects are above the surface

- Goals, terminology, structure
- Policies, procedures, products
- Financial resources

Covert aspects are below the surface

Benefits, assumptions, perceptions, attitudes, feelings, values, informal interactions, group works

McKinsey 7S

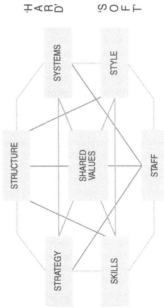

- **Structure**, **strategy** and **systems** are made up of facts and rules
- **Staff** have complex concerns and priorities
- **Skills** are core competences
- **Style** is management's methods, style and assumptions
- **Shared values** are guiding beliefs

'H A R D'

'S O F T'

All of the elements are **interlinked**. If any one variable is altered, the others will be affected.

Organisational ideologies (Harrison)

Harrison identified four types of organisation and described how they differed: **Structure** is an important aspect of this model. *Handy* popularised this model in *Gods of Management*: his names appear in brackets.

Power culture (Zeus)

In this culture power is centralised. Few rules or procedures exist and successful subordinates know what the power holders are likely to want. There is little concern for people within or without.

Role culture (Apollo)

The culture is formal, structured, procedural, impersonal and standardised. Members are risk averse and do not overstep their spheres of responsibility. This culture is efficient in a routine environment, less so in times of change.

Task culture (Athena)

In this culture the commitment is to achieving objectives. This culture uses teamwork and flexible approaches. Expertise is valued and the structure is flexible and changes rapidly.

Person culture (Dionysus)

The organisation exists to support its members or provide an arena for them to practise their skills and use their expertise. Administration as such is a low status role.

Miles and Snow

Strategic cultures

- **Defenders:** risk-averse, seek secure niche markets, emphasise correct procedure
- **Prospectors:** pursue results, seek to expand, pursue opportunities
- **Analysers:** balance risk and profit, build on a core of stable product-markets, follow prospectors into new markets
- **Reactors:** no real strategy, live from hand to mouth

Denison

Culture and the environment

Environmental response required	Internal		Strategic orientation	External
Stability		Consistency – bureaucracy		Mission eg a hospital
Change		Involvement – focus on motivation		Adaptability – eg a fashion company

Deal and Kennedy

'Strong' corporate cultures enhance performance via personal commitment to the norms and values of management. Culture can replace bureaucratic procedures as a means to get things done.

Cultures may be analysed into **four types**, according to **2 criteria**:

- **Degree of risk-taking** required in operations
- **Speed of feedback** of outcomes from decisions

Fast feedback

High risk

Bet your company

Long decision cycle, nerve and stamina needed (eg oil exploration)

Hard 'macho'

Seeks challenges (eg advertising, entertainment)

Process

Method, process, detail, status, risk management (eg banks)

Work hard/play hard

Team spirit, action fun (eg IT, any sales department)

Low risk

Slow feedback

The Hofstede model of national cultures

Hofstede pointed out that countries differ on the following dimensions.

a **Power distance.** This dimension measures how far superiors are expected to exercise power.

b **Uncertainty avoidance.** Some cultures prefer clarity and order, whereas others are prepared to accept novelty.

This affects the willingness of people to change rules, rather than simply obey them.

c **Individualism.** In some countries individual achievement is what matters. A collectivist culture puts the interests of the group first.

d **'Masculinity'.** In 'masculine' cultures, the roles of the sexes are clearly differentiated. 'Masculine' cultures emphasise possessions, status, and display as opposed to quality of life and concern for others.

Ouichi: Theory Z

Combines the best of US and Japanese cultural styles.

Hofstede grouped countries into eight clusters.

Group		Power distance	Uncertainty avoidance	Individualism	'Masculinity'
I	'More developed Latin'	High	High	Medium to high	Medium
II	'Less developed Latin'	High	High	Low	Whole range
III	'More developed Asian'	Medium	High	Medium	High
IV	'Less developed Asian'	High	Low to medium	Low	Medium
V	Near Eastern	High	High	Low	Medium
VI	'Germanic'	Low	Medium to high	Medium	Medium to high
VII	Anglo	Low to medium	Low to medium	High	High
VIII	Nordic	Low	Low to medium	Medium to high	Low

6: Communication, negotiation and conflict

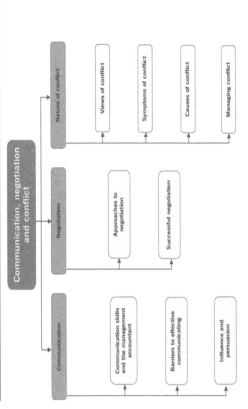

Communication, negotiation and conflict

Communication
- Communication skills and the management accountant
- Barriers to effective communicating
- Influence and persuasion

Negotiation
- Approaches to negotiation
- Successful negotiation

Nature of conflict
- Views of conflict
- Symptoms of conflict
- Causes of conflict
- Managing conflict

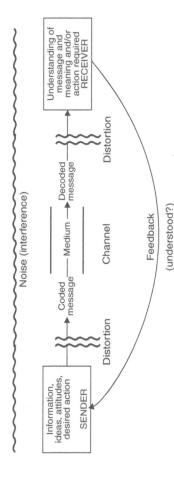

Negotiation

Communication

Conflict

The communication process

Noise (interference)

Information, ideas, attitudes, desired action
SENDER

Distortion

Coded message — Medium — Decoded message

Channel

Distortion

Understanding of message and meaning and/or action required
RECEIVER

Feedback
(understood?)

Communication in an organisation

Runs **vertically, horizontally** and **diagonally**

Oral communication skills include

- Appropriate language and usage
- Clear, audible, expressive, delivery
- Effective active, critical or empathetic listening

How to be an effective listener

- Be prepared to listen
- Be interested: listen ACTIVELY
- Be patient: wait your turn
- Keep an open mind: avoid prejudice
- Use your critical faculties
- Concentrate: don't get distracted/side-tracked
- Give feedback: encourage, ask, confirm
- Use non-verbal cues

Barriers to communication

- **Distortion or omission** by the sender
- **Unclear language** and use of jargon
- **Verbal and non-verbal contradiction**
- **Communication** overload
- **Mistrust and conflict**
- **Superfluous messages forgotten**
- **Lack of shared vocabulary**
- **Emotions**
- **Tendency to filter out the unwelcome message**

Written forms of communication provide a record of proposals, considerations and actions and can have the effect of concentrating the minds of both sender and receiver.

Letters: For external communication

Notice boards: For mass communication – must be managed to avoid staleness

Memoranda: For internal communication

House journals: To express corporate identity and report on developments

Forms: To enable the flow of routine information

Organisation manuals: Difficult to keep up to date in a dynamic environment but can be a good repository for information, rules and procedures

Questionnaires: To elicit information, especially in job and credit applications

Electronic communications: Email and voicemail; but ease of use can lead to overuse and misuse

A negotiation is a discussion between two parties who have different views on how an issue should be resolved. It differs from consultation in that both parties have a degree of power over the issue and therefore the outcome must be acceptable to them both.

Conventions of negotiation

- Both sides wish to reach a settlement
- Civilised behaviour is desirable
- Discussion may be off the record
- Firm offers and concessions should not be withdrawn
- Final agreements should be final

A negotiator should have an ideal outcome and a minimum acceptable outcome in mind.

Conducting a negotiation

1 Do not allow piecemeal settlement of parts of the issue

2 Any concession made should be matched by a concession received. This can be promoted by making conditional offers

3 Closing the negotiation
   - Offer a concession in exchange for settlement
   - Offer to split the difference on outstanding items
   - Offer a choice between two possibilities
   - Summarise arguments, emphasise concessions and make a final offer.

PREPARATION

Data gathering and analysis; Identifying key issues

Planning strategy and tactics; Preparing the meeting

OPENING

Opening

Presentation of each side's case

BARGAINING

Identifying common ground

Making concessions: moving together

CLOSING

Final offer

Conclusion

Constructive conflict

- Airs different solutions to problems
- Clarifies power structures
- Promotes the testing of ideas
- Releases hostile feelings
- Focuses attention on individual contributions

Destructive conflict

- Distracts attention from mission
- Polarises opinion
- Encourages political behaviour
- Can destroy the group
- Can lead to zero-sum conclusions

Vertical conflict

Arises between hierarchical levels, over such matters as work allocation, promotion, recognition and, particularly, over rewards. This is fertile ground for trade unions.

Horizontal conflict

Between individuals and groups at the same broad level in the organisation.

Causes of horizontal conflict between departments

- **Differences in goals**: Departmental goals must support the corporate mission, and where they appear to be in conflict with one another must be coordinated by senior management leadership. Note also that individual objectives must be congruent with departmental and corporate goals.

- **Personal differences of orientation** arise from personality, cultural influences and individual inclination. Leaders must play to people's strengths and integrate their efforts.

- **Task interdependence**: Departments rely on one another for the resources and information that make up workflows. It is possible for one department to disrupt the work performance of another by its inadequate performance.

- **Scarcity of resources**: Resources are always scarce and department heads compete for them.

- **Power structures** are rarely fixed and some managers will exploit opportunities to encroach on the prerogatives of others.

- **Uncertainty**: Stable operating conditions allow the development of harmonious, coordinated working practices. A changing, uncertain environment or an internal programme of change upsets accustomed practices, raises new problems and gives opportunities for the aggressive.

- The **reward system** must be fair as between staff in different departments.

Thomas' framework

Thomas uses this framework to classify different ways of handling conflict. It shows the behavioural style for handling conflict with (in brackets) the outcome sought.

Industrial relations

Conflict between management and trade unions over benefits and conditions is still endemic in some countries and some industries. Disputes have traditionally been tackled by **collective bargaining**. The relationship is formalised and made continuous in many EU countries by the use of **works councils** and **supervisory boards**. Some companies have taken an aggressive approach to union power.

Avoidance strategies include de-recognition of unions, moving to new non-union sites and single union, no-strike deals.

Human resource management strategies use an individualistic approach using single status; appraisal and performance management; profit sharing; and profit related pay.

Managing conflict

- Competitive (domination)   Collaborative (integration)

- Sharing (compromise)

                    Accommodative (appeasement) ●
- Avoidant (neglect) ●

(Unco-operative)   (Co-operative)

Desire to satisfy other party's concern

(Assertive)

(Unassertive)

Desire to satisfy own concern

Possible managerial responses to conflict

- **Avoidance:** It may be possible to ignore trivial incidents, though the causes of the conflict may erupt more violently later.
- **Accommodation:** This can be done with the use of exhortation and an emphasis on the need for teamwork.
- **Dominance:** Power can be applied to stamp out the dispute. This can create lingering resentment and hostility.
- **Compromise:** This can work, but splitting the difference can leave both parties unsatisfied. Also, they may exaggerate their opening positions if they expect to have to compromise.
- **Integration:** It may be possible to confront the issues and seek accommodation of differences by exploring the nature of the conflict.

Reduce conflict behaviour

- Structural separation
- Bureaucratic authority
- Limit communication

Reduce conflict behaviour

- Integration devices
- Confrontation and negotiation
- Staff exchanges
- Joint training
- Super-ordinate goals
- Analysis of causes
- Organisational adjustments
- Use consultants

7: Control and the finance function

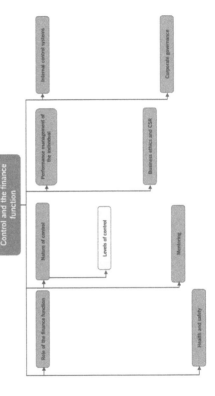

Types of control

Ouchi has identified 3 types of control:

- **Market control** assigns revenues and costs to profit centres and control is exercised via financial performance. It works well with autonomous trading units but not for centrally provided services.

- **Bureaucratic control** uses formal structures and procedures. It is impersonal, rational and efficient but relies on objective measurement. It is less useful where subjective impressions are important (eg where outputs are difficult to measure).

- **Cultural or clan control** works through shaping values, attitudes and commitment. It is useful for complex, abstruse or highly specialised work (such as research) where outputs are difficult to measure or to price.

Personal centralised control *Ouchi*'s work on control strategies can be extended to include a form of control known as personal centralised control. It is often found in owner-managed organisations. Its key feature is a central figure who acts as the main decision-maker in the organisation. Control is achieved over activities by the owner personally overseeing the work of employees.

A major function of organisation structure is the provision of a mechanism through which control can be exercised. A feedback or cybernetic control system works like this.

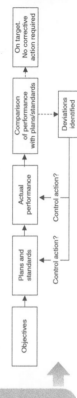

Control system

Objectives → Plans and standards → Actual performance → Comparison of performance with plans/standards → On target. No corrective action required

Control action? — Control action? — Control action?

Deviations identified

Levels of control (*Anthony*)

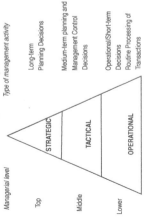

Managerial level	Type of management activity
Top	Long-term Planning Decisions
Middle	Medium-term planning and Management Control Decisions
Lower	Operational/Short-term Decisions Routine Processing of Transactions

STRATEGIC

TACTICAL

OPERATIONAL

Control strategies and processes

Ouchi. Three basic **control strategies** are used in organisations.

Market control

Bureaucratic control

Clan control

Johnson and Scholes. Two types of control processes exist in organisations

Input-focused or **output-focused**

Direct or **indirect**

Effective control systems

For control systems to be effective they must satisfy **six criteria.**

Acceptability

Accessability

Adaptability

Action orientation

Appropriateness

Affordability

Internal control systems

Turnbull Report

Suggests that internal controls are **policies, processes, tasks, behaviour** and other aspects that:

Facilitate **effective** and **efficient operation**

Help ensure quality of **internal and external reporting**

Help ensure **compliance** with laws and regulations.

The role of the finance function

Responsibilities

- Allocation and effective use of resources
- Reporting results (financial accounting)
- Analysing performance (management accounting)
- Evaluating investments
- Providing information to stakeholders

Measures of success

- Provision of reliable, relevant information
- Flexibility
- Speed of reporting
- Efficiency
- Balanced scorecard

Stakeholder relationships

- **Internal** – relevant information for those who need it
- **Business advisers** – information required for advice
- **Auditors** – external/internal audit links
- **Investors** – results and financial management
- **Financiers** – details of profits and liquidity

Business partner model

The business partner model has been developed in response to criticisms that the finance function is too concerned with control and past performance. Gives finance function a more active role in providing information, and expands its role to cover strategic issues such as investment.

Outsourcing

Outsourcing of basic transaction processing and payroll management is now common, with the finance function concentrating on provision of key information. Alternative is use of shared service centres.

Problems with business partner model

- Loss of independence
- Too identified with operational managers
- Failure to provide sufficient control
- Lack of focus on providing true and fair view external stakeholders require

Independent business partner

Finance function's role is to add value not create it. The finance function's focus should be on the safeguarding of assets and effective reporting, rigorous assessment and validation of strategic ideas.

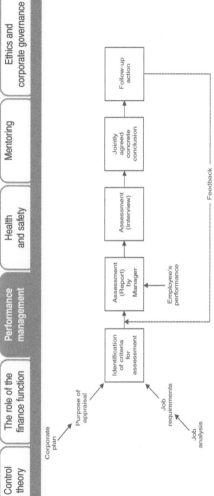

Appraisal techniques

Overall assessment in narrative form: value depends on quality of writing and **guidance** on standards and what to cover.

Grading using numerical or graphical **rating scales** for specified characteristics.

Behavioural incident methods give examples of behaviour for each grade and characteristic.

Results oriented schemes review performance against specific targets previously agreed between appraiser and appraisee.

Appraisal

is the systematic review and assessment of an employee's performance, potential and training needs.

Reasons for formal appraisal

- Force managers to undertake a full and rational review rather than relying on random impressions

- Force managers to give adequate feedback to subordinates

- Force managers to consider development needs and potential for promotion

Purposes of appraisal

- **Performance review**: feedback on performance and identification of training or development needs

- **Reward review**: assess appropriateness of pay increases and bonuses

- **Potential review**: more senior staff are best placed to assess potential

The appraisal interview

Maier identifies 3 approaches:

Tell and sell: manager announces assessment and tries to gain acceptance of verdict and improvement plan.

Tell and listen: manager announces assessment but invites response and discussion.

Problem-solving: manager acts as counsellor to assist employee's self development.

Managers should be **well prepared** for the appraisal interview since it can be stressful for both participants. Training and pay implications and possibilities should be researched in advance.

Any agreed action should be **followed up** to ensure that it happens.

Appraisal schemes

- **Traditional schemes** rely on the assessment of employees by their managers.

- **Self appraisal** saves management time and can enhance employee commitment.

- **Upward appraisal** of managers by employees brings an important new perspective, especially where there is a high degree of consistency of opinion.

- **360° appraisal** extends this principle by seeking input from peers and co-workers, customers (including internal 'customers') and the appraisees themselves.

Appraisal barriers

- Potential for **confrontation and hostility** based on disagreements on role, performance, objectivity and presentation.

- **Inadequate participation** by appraisees who see the process as over-judgmental.

- **Lack of firmness** by appraisers who avoid criticism and achieve little.

- **Bureaucratic, time bound, paper based nature** of the appraisal process interferes with its real purpose.

- Failure to **incorporate appraisal into a wider spectrum** of continuing performance management.

- Agreed **targets** become **irrelevant** as time passes if appraisals are no more frequent than annually.

Legal framework

Legislation governing health and safety at work:

Health and Safety at Work Act 1974

The Management of Health and Safety at Work Regulations 1992

Health and Safety (Consultation with Employees) Regulations 1996

The Workplace (Health, Safety and Welfare) Regulations 1992

The Manual Handling Operations Regulations 1992

The Health and Safety (Display Screen Equipment) Regulations 1992

Working Time Regulations 1998

The Health and Safety Executive (HSE)

The Health and Safety Executive (HSE) is an independent body responsible for encouraging and enforcing employers to comply with the Health and Safety at Work Act.

The impact of health and safety

Accidents and illness increase costs.
Public image is influenced.
Employers have **legal obligations.**

Employees' duties

- Take reasonable care of themselves and others
- Allow the employer to carry out his duties, including enforcing safety rules
- Use equipment properly
- Report potential hazards
- Not interfere recklessly with machinery or equipment

UK legislation

Employers' duties

- **Work practices** must be safe
- **Work environment** must be safe and healthy
- **Risk assessments** must be carried out
- **At-risk employees** must be identified
- **Health and safety advisers** must be competent
- Plant and equipment must be **maintained** to the proper standard
- **Training and information** to encourage **safe working practices** should be provided
- **Controls** should reduce risks
- **Safety policies** should be introduced and regularly revised

Mentoring

Mentoring is a broad activity, comprising career building functions, such as sponsorship, coaching and protection; and psycho-social functions such as providing a role model, counselling, friendship and creating a sense of acceptance and belonging.

Ethics

Ethics are the moral principles by which people act or do business.

Two ethical values are pertinent for business: **ordinary decency** and **distributive justice.**

Ethical problems

- Extortion by officials
- Bribery
- Unfair competition
- Product safety
- Honesty in advertising
- Environmental impact

Social responsibility

It is commonly expected that business will provide benefits to society generally, not just by economic activity or to specific stakeholder groups; legislation and social and political pressure promote this now.

- **Employment:** in many countries, equal opportunities and employment protection legislation hampers businesses' ability to adjust the size of their workforce and control labour costs.

- **Environmental and externalities:** extensive legislation is designed to protect the natural environment and other forms of amenity such as health and family life.

Promoting ethical behaviour – two approaches

	Compliance	Integrity
Ethos	Conform with imposed standards	Choose ethical standards
Objective	Keep to the law	Enable legal and responsible conduct
Originators	Lawyers	Management
Methods	Reduced employee discretion	Leadership, education, systems
Behavioural assumptions	People are solitary self-interested beings	People are social beings with values
Standards	The law	Ethical values and the law
Education	The law, compliance system	Values, the law, compliance systems

Whichever approach is chosen, it will be ineffective if senior managers set a bad example.

Fundamental principles of CIMA's code of ethics

- CIMA's Code of Ethics is based on the International Federation of Accountants (IFAC) Code of Ethics.

- **Integrity** is more than not telling lies; professional accountants must not be party to anything which is deceptive or misleading.

- **Objectivity** is founded on fairness and avoiding all forms of bias, prejudice and partiality.

- **Professional competence and due care.**

- **Confidentiality.** Employers and clients are entitled to expect that confidential information will not be revealed without specific permission or unless there is a legal or professional right or duty to do so.

- **Professional behaviour** protects the reputation of the professional and the professional body.

Corporate governance is the system by which organisations are directed and controlled. Most countries have compliance codes on corporate governance.

Failures of corporate governance

There have always been swindles. There have been several very large ones:

- Polly Peck
- Robert Maxwell
- BCCI
- Enron
- Parmalat
- World Com

Good corporate governance

- Reduces risk
- Improves performance
- Improves external perceptions

The UK Stock Exchange Corporate Governance Code

The code lays down best practice for the way large companies should be run. Among its provisions are these:

- **Directors** should use independent judgement; the roles of Chairman and CEO should be separate; no individual or group should dominate; there should be a balance of executive and non-executive directors.

- **Director's remuneration** should be subject to formal and clear procedure and largely controlled by non-executive directors.

- Non-executive directors' **audit committee** should oversee both internal and external audit.

8: Change management

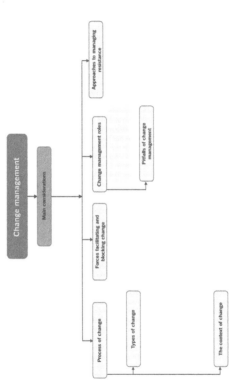

Change management

Main considerations

Process of change

Types of change

The context of change

Forces facilitating and blocking change

Change management roles

Pitfalls of change management

Approaches to managing resistance

The management of change starts with an understanding of three main considerations.

1 **The type of change** required – its scope and nature

Scope of change

		Realignment	Transformation
Nature of change	Incremental	Adaptation	Evolution
	'Big bang'	Reconstruction	Revolution

2 **The wider context of the change**, in large part cultural considerations

- **Time** available
- Features to **preserve**
- Organisational **diversity**
- **Capability** to manage change
  - Largely depends on experience

- **Capacity** – Availability of resources, especially finance, IS/IT and management effort
- Workforce **readiness** to change, or resistence to change
- **Power** to effect change
- **Scope** of change needed

3 **Forces facilitating and blocking change** – use of force field analysis

Beer and Nohria – Theory E & Theory O

Beer and Nohria suggest that although each organisation's change is unique, each change is ultimately a variant of two underlying approaches. Beer and Nohria call these underlying approaches **Theory E'** and **Theory O'**.

Theory E: the basis of change is to increase economic value. Theory E change usually involves the use of economic incentives, drastic layoffs, downsizing and restructuring.

Drawbacks of Theory E:

- Ignores the feelings of employees
- May reduce motivation and commitment
- Loss of creativity

Theory O: aims to develop human capability to implement strategy, and to develop corporate culture through organisational learning. The process is participative (rather than being top down) with an emphasis on feedback and reflection.

Drawbacks of Theory O:

- Encourages managers to avoid taking difficult decisions

There are five main styles of change management:

Style	Characterised by	Appropriate to
1 Education and communication	Persuasion	Incremental change, willing staff
2 Collaboration and participation	Involving those affected	Incremental change, supportive culture
3 Intervention	Change agents	Incremental change
4 Direction	Managerial authority, probability of resistance	Transformation
5 Coercion/edict	Use of power to impose change	Times of crisis

Different approaches may be appropriate to different stakeholders. Normal management practice will also affect the style used. It may be advantageous to use more than one style.

Kotter and Schlesinger identify six approaches to overcoming staff resistance:

- Education and communication
- Participation and involvement
- Facilitation and support
- Negotiation and agreement
- Manipulation and co-operation
- Coercion, implicit and explicit

A **change agent** is an individual or group that helps to bring about strategic change in an organisation.

Johnson, Scholes and Whittington examine change agency by considering three distinct groups:

1 **Strategic leaders**

Five approaches to strategic leadership:

- **Strategic analysis** and design focus
- **Human assets** development focus
- **Expertise** as source of competitive advantage focus
- **Control** by procedures and performance monitoring
- **Change** as continuous process – emphasis on communication and monitoring

2 **Middle management**

Providers of advice; translation of strategy at local level; implementation and control

3 **Outsiders**

Bringing a fresh point of view, such as a new chief executive or the use of consultants

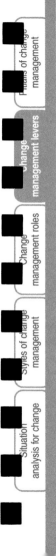

A **turnaround strategy** is required when a business is in **terminal decline**. It has its own change management techniques:

Crisis stabilisation – management changes – communication with stakeholders – attention to target markets – concentration of effort – financial restructuring – prioritisation

In other circumstances, change management levers relate to the **cultural web**.

Change management levers

Challenging the paradigm	move away from entrenched habits
Changing routines	discard old ways of doing things
Use of symbolic processes	introduce new rituals and systems
Power and politics	build a power base, overcome resistance and achieve compliance
Communication and monitoring	explain the need for change, what change intends to achieve
Tactics	careful timing, use of 'quick wins', handling job losses – with care.

Change programmes may be **subverted** and lead to **unintended consequences**. This has four implications for change management.

- **Monitoring** and **control** are vital.
- The existing **culture** must be understood.
- The organisation's **people** should be involved in the change process.
- The **extent** of the challenge must be recognised.

9a: Project management – Part A

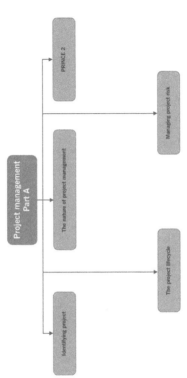

Project management Part A

- Identifying project
- The nature of project management
- PRINCE 2
- The project lifecycle
- Managing project risk

Projects

A project is 'an undertaking that has a beginning and an end, and is carried out to meet established goals within cost, schedule and quality objectives.'
Haynes, Project Management

Characteristics of a project

- A defined beginning and end
- Resources allocated specifically
- Follow a plan towards a clear intended end result
- Often cut across organisational lines
- Often unique or seldom done

Project management

Integration of all aspects of a project, ensuring that the proper knowledge and resources are available when and where needed, and above all to ensure that the expected outcome is produced in a timely, cost-effective manner. The primary function of a project manager is to manage the trade-offs between performance, timeliness and cost. (*CIMA*)

The US Project Management Institute guide to the Project Management Body of Knowledge lists nine key knowledge areas that support five project management process areas.

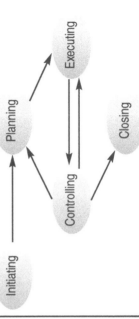

Project management process areas

Initiating

Planning

Executing

Controlling

Closing

Key project management knowledge areas

- Integration
- Cost
- Communications
- Scope
- Quality
- Risk
- Time
- Human resources
- Procurement

9a: Project management – Part A

Feasibility studies

Technical feasibility

- Requirement for **innovation** or **development**?
- Expertise available?
- **Non-technological** techniques such as marketing?
- **Features analysis** identifies critical features of requirement so as to guide resource allocation.

Environmental concerns

Mostly about **acceptability**.

Social feasibility

Consider effects on groups and individuals both inside and outside the organisation and even on society as a whole.

Financial feasibility

Normal techniques such as NPV are used. Difficulties arise in valuing intangible benefits: this is particularly a problem in the public and voluntary sectors.

Projects are only undertaken for good reason

1. Projects are initiated in order to achieve objectives that cannot be attained in any other way.

2. A project's objective may be referred to as the **project requirement**: the **project specification** is a detailed account of the nature of the project or the outcomes it is intended to deliver.

3. Projects to achieve strategic objectives are strategies and should be assessed using the **suitability**, **acceptability** and **feasibility** criteria.

4. **Feasibility** is particularly important and may be assessed by a **feasibility study**. The aim is to avoid commitment to projects whose benefits will be outweighed by their overall costs.

PRINCE

PRINCE is a project management system developed by the UK *Central Computer and Telecommunications Agency*.

The acronym PRINCE stands for **PR**ojects **IN** Controlled Environments. The latest version of PRINCE is PRINCE2.

Main features of PRINCE2

- **Scaleable system** can be used to manage projects of any size and complexity
- Defines a **clear management structure** of roles and responsibilities
- Focuses on **delivering products** rather than on project management processes
- **Business case** is fundamental: continuing viability checked regularly

PRINCE2 components

- **Business case:** a reasoned account of what is to be achieved and why it will be of benefit; may require updating as project progresses

- **Plans:** based on products rather than processes; product breakdown structure is used

- **Controls:** normal feedback control is used; project board restricts approval to one step at a time

- **Risk:** analysed, managed and reviewed throughout the project's life

- **Quality:** built into management, though not a quality management system as such

- **Change control:** manages authorised changes to the project

- **Configuration management:** *configuration* is a complete specification of what is needed to complete the project; configuration management controls the processes by which the project's intended products evolve

- **Organisation:** four layers of management cover all eventualities; layers may be combined for smaller projects and organisations

PRINCE2 processes

- **Directing a project:** higher aspects of control and decision-making
- **Starting up a project:** short, pre-project; fundamentals such as setting aims
- **Initiating a project:** initial planning, QA and setting of progress and such criteria
- **Planning:** based on product breakdown structure starting with analysis into **technical**, **quality** and **management** products; tolerances may be established for targets of time, cost and quality
- **Controlling a stage:** project board uses project initiation meeting, mid and end stage assessments, highlight reports; project team uses **checkpoints** to control progress
- **Managing stage boundaries:** ensures one stage is complete before the next begins
- **Managing product delivery:** controls the work done by specialists and contractors
- **Closing a project:** checks and reports on success *via* a project closure meeting

The 4D model

Stage in project lifecycle	Component	Activities
Define the project	Conceptualisation	Produce a clear and definitive statement of needs
	Analysis	Identify what has to be done and check its feasibility
Design the project	Planning Justification Agreement	Show how the needs will be met Compute costs and benefit Obtain sponsor agreement
Deliver the project	Start up Execution Completion	Assemble resources and people Carry out planned project activities Success or abandonment
Develop the process	Review Feedback	Identify outcomes for all stakeholders Document lessons and improvements for future

Risk management

Risk management involves an overview of the project to establish what could go wrong, and the consequences.

Five stages of risk management

- Identify and record risks in a risk register
- Assess risks and record this assessment
- Plan and record risk strategies
- Carry out risk management strategies
- Review and monitor the success of the risk management approach.

The likelihood and consequences of risks can be plotted on a matrix.

Risk Assessment Matrix

Potential impact	Low	Med	High
High	M	H	VH
Med	L	M	H
Low	VL	L	M

The development of risk management strategies for risks that fall into the VH (Very High) quadrant should have priority.

Dealing with risk involves four basic approaches (a combination of these approaches may be used).

Dealing with risk

- **Avoidance** – remove the factors bringing about the risk.
- **Reduction** – identify ways to reduce the risk and/or consequences.
- **Transference** – pass the risk to someone else, for example an insurer.
- **Absorption** – accept the risk and cope with the consequences if necessary.

9b: Project management – Part B

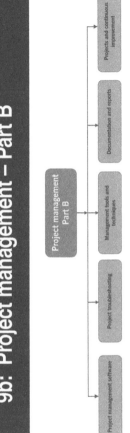

Project management Part B
- Project management software
- Project troubleshooting
- Management tools and techniques
- Documentation and reports
- Projects and continuous improvement

Work breakdown structure (WBS)

Work breakdown structure is the analysis of the work of a project into different units or tasks.

WBS:

- Identifies the work that must be done in the project
- Determines the resources required
- Sequences the work done, to allocate resources in the optimum way

WBS can be used in devising estimates. From the WBS it is possible to compile a complete list of every task that is going to attract expenditure.

Dependencies and interactions

- A **dependent** task cannot commence until the task upon which it depends is completed. Analysis of dependencies shows the order in which tasks must be carried out.

- Tasks **interact** when they cannot be carried out at the same time, for example, because they require the use of same resources.

The Project Budget

The **project budget** records the amount and distribution of resources allocated to a project.

Top-down budgeting describes the situation where the budget is imposed 'from above'.

In **bottom-up** budgeting the project manager consults the project team, and others, to calculate a budget based on the tasks that make up the project.

Improving estimates
■ Learn from past mistakes
■ Analyse the project properly
■ Obtain maximum information
■ Specify in maximum detail

Influences on cost
■ Level of quality required
■ External vendor activity
■ Staff availability
■ Degree of time constraint

Gantt charts

A Gantt chart is a **horizontal bar chart used** to plan the time scale for a project and to estimate the amount of resources required. The Gantt chart displays the time relationships between tasks in a project. Two lines are used for each task, one to show the planned time, the other to show the actual time.

An example of a simple Gantt chart, relating to a network server installtation project, is shown below.

The chart shows that at the end of the tenth week, Activity 9 is running behind schedule. More resources may have to be allocated to this activity if the staff accommodation is to be ready in time for the changeover to the new system.

Activity 4 had not been completed on time, and this has resulted in some disruption to the computer installation (Activity 6), which may mean further delays in the commencement of Activities 7 and 8.

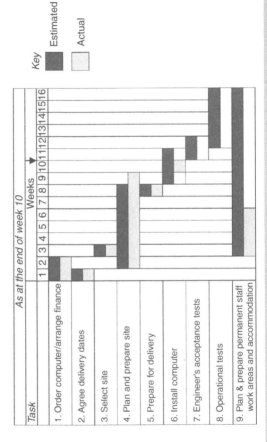

As at the end of week 10

Task	Weeks

Key: Estimated / Actual

1. Order computer/arrange finance
2. Agree delivery dates
3. Select site
4. Plan and prepare site
5. Prepare for delivery
6. Install computer
7. Engineer's acceptance tests
8. Operational tests
9. Plan & prepare permanent staff work areas and accommodation

9b: Project management – Part B

Drawing the diagram or chart involves the following steps.

1 Estimating the time needed to complete each individual activity or task that makes up a part of the project.

2 Sorting out what activities must be done one after another, and which can be done at the same time, if required.

3 Representing these in a network diagram.

4 Estimating the critical path, which is the longest sequence of consecutive activities through the network.

Activities on the critical path must be started and completed on time, otherwise the total project time will be extended.

Network analysis or CPA

Network analysis (CPA) is a useful technique to help with **planning** and **controlling large projects.**

It starts with **breaking down the project into tasks,** arranging them into a **logical sequence** and estimating the **duration** of each.

This enables the **series of tasks** that determines the **minimum possible duration** of the project to be found. These are the **critical activities.**

Events (usually numbers) are represented by circles. Tasks (usually letters) connect events.

The **critical path** is represented by drawing an extra line or a thicker line between the tasks on the path.

Example

Activity	Expected time	Preceding activity
A	3	–
B	5	–
C	2	B
D	1	A
E	6	A
F	3	D
G	3	C, E

Critical path and **float times** are established by the forward and rearward passes through the network.

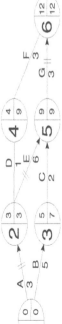

Key

Event number

Earliest start time for next task

Latest start time for next task

The diagrams are drawn from left to right.

The critical path in the diagram above is AEG. Note the **float time** of five days for Activity F. Activity F can begin any time between days 4 and 9.

Activity-on-node presentation

Network diagrams may also be drawn using activity-on-node presentation.

Suppose that a project includes three activities, C, D and E. Neither activity D nor E can start until activity C is completed, but D and E could be done simultaneously if required.

This would be represented as follows.

An activity within a network is represented by a rectangular box. (Each box is a node.)

The flow of activities in the diagram should be from left to right.

The diagram clearly shows that D and E must follow C.

One way of showing earliest and latest start times for activities is to divide each event node into sections, as shown below.

Task D	
ID number: 4	**Duration:** 6 days
Earliest start: Day 4	**Latest start:** Day 11

To find the **earliest start times**, always start with activities that have no predecessors and give them an earliest starting time of 0.

Then work along each path from **left** to **right** through the diagram calculating the earliest time that the next activity can start.

If two or more activities precede an activity take the highest figure as the later activity's earliest start time: it cannot start before all the others are finished!

The **latest start times** are the latest times at which each activity can start if the project as a whole is to be completed in the earliest possible time.

Criticisms of network analysis

- It is not always possible to devise an effective WBS for a project.

- It assumes a sequential relationship between activities.

- There are problems in estimation.

- CPA assumes a trade-off between time and cost. This may not be the case where a substantial portion of the cost is indirect.

Project evaluation review technique (PERT)

Project evaluation and review technique (PERT) is a technique for allowing for uncertainty in determining project duration.

Each task is assigned a **best**, **worst**, and **most probable completion time** estimate. These estimates are used to determine the average completion time. The average times are used to establish the critical path and the standard deviation of completion times for the entire project.

A contingency time allowance can then be calculated, based on the standard deviations of the times for each critical activity.

Critical chain project management (CCPM)

CCPM attempts to overcome problems of **padding** and **delays** inherent in network analysis and WBS.

It does this in three ways. First of all it does this by preventing padding of **time estimates**. Then, by building **margins of safety** in at the final project stage to cover the accumulated overruns. Finally, by emphasising flexibility in responding to changes. **Buffers** are also used.

Resource histogram

Shows the amount and timing of the requirement for a resource or a range of resources.

A simple resource histogram showing the programmer time required on a software development program is shown here.

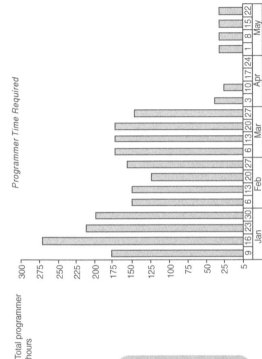

Programmer Time Required

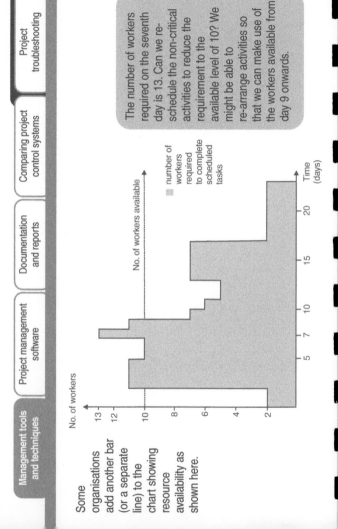

Some organisations add another bar (or a separate line) to the chart showing resource availability as shown here.

No. of workers available

No. of workers

■ number of workers required to complete scheduled tasks

The number of workers required on the seventh day is 13. Can we re-schedule the non-critical activities to reduce the requirement to the available level of 10? We might be able to re-arrange activities so that we can make use of the workers available from day 9 onwards.

Project management software

Project management software packages have been available for a number of years. **Microsoft Project** and **Micro Planner X-Pert** are two popular packages.

Software might be used for a number of purposes.

- **Planning** – network diagrams (showing the critical path) and Gantt charts (showing resource use) can be produced automatically once the relevant data is entered.
- **Monitoring** – actual data can also be entered and used to facilitate monitoring of progress and automatically update network diagrams.
- **Estimating** – since many projects involve basically similar tasks, actual data from one project can be used to provide more accurate estimates for the next project.
- **Reporting** – software packages allow standard and tailored progress reports to be produced.

Any project management package requires four inputs:

- The length of time required for each activity of the project
- The logical relationships between each activity
- The resources available
- When the resources are available

Documentation and reports

The project charter (project brief, project initiation document) gives project board approval for the project manager to apply resources to project activities. It also contains the terms of reference for the project.

Project plan

In some organisations what is described here as the **Project Management Plan** would be called the **Project Plan**.

In other organisations, the Project Plan refers only to the project schedule, usually in the form of a network diagram.

The Project Plan is used as a reference tool for managing the project. The plan is used to guide both project execution and project control.

The project plan should include:

- Project objectives and how they will be achieved and verified
- How any changes to these procedures are to be controlled
- The management and technical procedures, and standards, to be used
- The budget and time-scale
- Safety, health and environmental policies
- Inherent risks and how they will be managed

The contents of the plan will vary depending on the complexity of the project.

Progress report

A progress report shows the current status of the project, usually in relation to the planned status.

```
Progress reports

■ Frequency and contents will vary depending on project complexity
■ They are a control tool
■ They should monitor progress towards key milestones
```

A milestone is a significant event in the project, usually completion of a major deliverable.

Completion report

The completion report summarises the results of the project, and includes client sign-off. The report should include a summary of the project outcome.

Completion report should contain

- Project objectives and the outcomes achieved
- The final project budget report showing expected and actual expenditure (if an external client is involved this information may be sensitive – the report may exclude or 'amend' the budget report).
- A brief outline of time taken compared with the original schedule

The completion report will also include provision for any ongoing issues that will need to be addressed after completion. Such issues would be related to the project, but not part of the project.

Post-completion audit

The post-completion audit is a formal review of the project that examines the lessons that may be learned and used for the benefit of future projects.

The audit looks at all aspects with regard to:

1. Did the end result of the project meet with the **client's expectations**?

   - The actual design and construction of the end product
   - Was the project achieved on time?
   - Was the project completed within budget?

2. Was the **management of the project** as successful as it might have been, or were there bottlenecks or problems?

   This review covers:

   - Problems that might occur on future projects with similar characteristics
   - The performance of the team individually and as a group

   This information should be formalised in a report.

PMBOK v PRINCE 2

Read 'Comparing PRINCE 2 with PMBOK' by R Max Wideman

Six Sigma

D efine

M easure

A nalyse

I mprove

C ontrol

An **operating system** for measuring and eliminating faults through promoting excellence.

The relationship between time, cost and quality can be shown as a triangle.

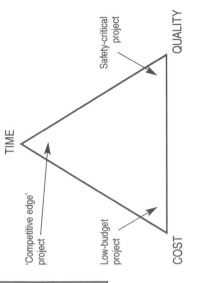

Common causes of problems on projects

- Poor project management
- Conflicting requirements (eg time, cost and quality)
- Unrealistic deadline
- User requirements not established correctly

When a project has slipped behind schedule there are a range of options open to the project manager.

Dealing with slippage

- **Do nothing**
  After considering all options, it may be decided to let things continue as they are.

- **Add resources**
  Add people or other resources.

- **Work smarter**
  Could more efficient methods be used?

- **Replan**
  A more realistic plan may be required.

- **Reschedule**
  A complete replan may not be required – it may be possible to change the phasing of certain deliverables.

- **Incentives**
  Would incentives result in greater output?

- **Change the specification**
  If the original project objectives are unrealistic given the time and money available, it may be necessary to change the specification.

Project change procedure

Causes of change to the Project Plan

- Slippage
- Availability of new technology
- Changes in personnel
- Poorly defined user requirements
- New legislation
- Business environment changes

Considerations when changing the Plan

- Consequences of not implementing the change
- Impact on time, cost, quality
- Costs and benefits of the change
- Risks
- Impact on stakeholders
- Change control procedure
- Communication to all affected

Projects and continuous improvement

Continuous improvement applies to projects especially where they become a routine means of working in organisations.

- Project management can be a core strategic competence for companies working in such industries as consulting and construction.

- Continuous improvement requires that project management is placed at the centre of a single corporate methodology. This involves developing an organisational culture which supports the need for continuous improvement.

10: The project team

The project team

- Roles and management of project stakeholders
- Projects and organisational structure
- Leading, managing and motivating teams
- The project manager

The project manager

The person who takes ultimate responsibility for ensuring a project achieves the desired result on-time, within budget and to specification, is the project manager (PM).

PM responsibilities to management

- Use resources efficiently
- Keep management informed
- Adhere to agreed policies and procedures

PM responsibilities to the project and to the project team

- Keep the project on target
- Ensure required resources are available
- Co-ordinate the team
- Provide support

Duties of a project manager

- Project planning and scheduling
- Communication and teambuilding
- Monitoring and control (eg budgeting)
- Problem and conflict resolution
- Quality control

To perform these duties well a project manager requires well developed communication, technical and personal skills.

The
project manager

Projects
and structure

Project
stakeholders

The
project team

Team meetings
and conflict

Pure project organisation

Central permanent organisation

Flexible ad-hoc labour force

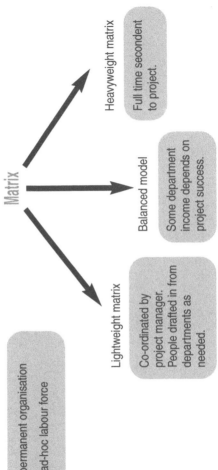

Matrix

Heavyweight matrix

Full time secondent to project.

Balanced model

Some department income depends on project success.

Lightweight matrix

Co-ordinated by project manager. People drafted in from departments as needed.

Project stakeholders

Stakeholders are the individuals and organisations who are involved in or may be affected by project activities.

Other key stakeholders

- **Project sponsor:** is accountable for the resources invested into the project and responsible for the achievement of the project's business objectives.
- **Project Board:** the body to which the project manager is accountable for achieving the project objectives.
- **Project support team:** is a term used to designate the personnel working on a project who do not report to the project manager administratively.
- **Users:** the individual or group that will utilise the end product, process (system), or service produced by the project.

The role of the management accountant in project work

The skills of the management accountant are well suited to supporting project teams as they are able to monitor project progress from a financial perspective.

The management accountant can support the project team in a number of ways:

- Conducting cost – benefit analysis
- Producing project budgets and forecasts
- Updating the project accounting system
- Maintaining a complete project audit trail
- Making stage payments to project supplies
- Monitoring and investigating budget variances
- Liasing with the project sponsor

Mendelow: Stakeholder mapping

Stakeholders' interests are likely to conflict.

Mendelow's **stakeholder mapping** helps the organisation to establish its priorities and set up its system of corporate governance.

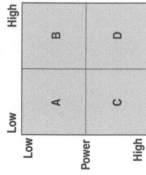

Level of interest

	Low	High
Low	A	B
High	C	D

Power (rows: Low, High)

A: **Minimal effort**

B: **Keep informed**; little direct influence but may influence more powerful stakeholders

C: Treat with care; often passive but capable of moving to segment D; **keep satisfied**

D: **Key players** – strategy must be **acceptable** to them, at least

Groups and teams

A **group** differs from a random collection of people in that its members perceive themselves to be a group. They have:

- A sense of identity
- Loyalty to the group
- Purpose and leadership

A team is more than a group having objectives and accountability

Types of groups

Four types of group are commonly found in most organisations, these include:

- **Formal groups** are created by managers to meet specific organisational objectives
- **Informal groups** develop out of individual relationships and are based on shared interests
- **Reference groups** are those that a person wants to join but is not currently a member of
- **Autonomous working groups** are experiments in improving productivity by getting individuals to work in small cells or teams

Development of the team (*Tuckman*)

1 **Forming.** The team is still a collection of individuals jockeying for position. Aims, norms and personalities are probably unclear and no leader is likely to have emerged.

2 **Storming.** There may be open conflict as objectives and norms are set and revised. Trust increases.

3 **Norming.** The team settles down and creates norms for output, worksharing and individual needs.

4 **Performing.** The team is sufficiently integrated to perform its task.

Building a project team

The project team comprises the people who report directly or indirectly to the project manager.

Project success depends to a large extent on the team of members selected. The team will comprise individuals with differing skills and personalities.

The **project manager** should choose a balanced team that takes advantage of each team member's skills and compensates elsewhere for their weaknesses.

The **project team** will normally be drawn from existing staff, but highly recommended outsiders with special skills may be recruited.

Multidisciplinary team

Members have different skills, knowledge and experience.
Such teams can solve problems with cross-disciplinary aspects.

Multi-skilled team

Members all have a range of skills, enabling greater flexibility of work patterns.

Managing the project team

Effective project managers display the ability to:

- Select the right people
- Connect them to the right cause
- Solve problems that arise
- Evaluate progress towards objectives
- Negotiate resolutions to conflicts
- Heal wounds inflicted by change

Project team structure

Three ways of structuring projects:

- Functional structure
- Matrix Structure
- Process (pure project) structure

Team roles (*Belbin*)

Effective teams have members who between them are capable of fulfilling nine vital roles:

- **Co-ordinator**
  Presides and co-ordinates; balanced, disciplined, good at working through others. Mature and confident.

- **Shaper**
  Highly strung, dominant, extrovert, passionate about the task itself, a spur to action.

- **Plant**
  Introverted, but intellectually dominant and imaginative; source of ideas and proposals but with disadvantages of introversion.

- **Monitor-evaluator**
  Analytically (rather than creatively) intelligent; dissects ideas, spots flaws; judges accurately.

- **Resource-investigator**
  Sociable, extrovert, relaxed; source of new contacts, but not an originator; explores opportunities.

- **Implementer**
  Practical organiser, turning ideas into tasks; trustworthy and efficient, but not excited.

- **Team worker**
  Supportive, understanding, diplomatic; popular, uncompetitive and mild.

- **Completer**
  Attends to details and delivery; conscientious and anxious.

- **Specialist**
  Dedicated, knowledgeable, single minded.

Rewarding effective teams

Team-based rewards and incentives may be used to encourage co-operation and mutual accountability, as well as team performance.

Characteristics of effective and ineffective teams

Factor	Effective teams	Ineffective teams
Quantifiable		
Labour turnover	Low	High
Absenteeism	Low	High
Quality of output	High	Low
Individual targets	Met	Not met
Qualitative		
Commitment to organisational goals	High	Low
Communication between team members	Free and open	Mistrust
Job satisfaction	High	Low

Team meetings

Meetings are an important mechanism of team communication and collaboration.

Purpose

- Opportunity to **review team working**
- **Reinforce team sense** as a team
- **Goal reinforcement**
- **Involvement in decision making** by team members
- **Informal communication**

Effective meetings

Whetten and **Cameron** give five attributes of effective meetings, classified as five P's.

- Purpose
- Participants
- Planning
- Process
- Perspective

The project manager	Projects and structure	Project stakeholders	The project team

The **project team** should include people who, between them, can deploy all of the skills and talents needed for the project.

Managing conflict

It is inevitable when people from wide-ranging backgrounds combine to form a project team that conflict will occasionally occur.

Ideally, conflict should be harnessed for productive ends.

Negotiation techniques

- Focus on the problem, not the personalities
- Define the problem carefully
- Try to develop options that would result in mutual gain
- Look for a wide variety of possible solutions

Resolution techniques

- Work through the problem using the negotiation techniques listed above
- Attempt to establish a compromise
- Try to smooth out any differences
- Emphasise areas of agreement
- If all else fails, the project manager should force the issue and make a decision

Positive effects of conflict

- Results in better, well thought-out ideas
- Forces people to search for new approaches
- Causes persistent problems to surface and be dealt with
- Forces people to clarify their views
- Causes tension which stimulates interest and creativity

Notes

Notes